NEW AND CLASSIC

COCKTAILS

WITHOUT ALCOHOL

Dhahran 7/94

NEW AND CLASSIC

COCKTAILS

WITHOUT ALCOHOL

ROBERT SUTTON AND KEITH POINTING

PHOTOGRAPHY BY VERNON MORGAN

STACEY INTERNATIONAL

Editor
John Blackett-Ord
Designer
Keith Pointing
Design Assistant
Celeste Henney
Photographer
Vernon Morgan
Home Economists
Ricky Turner, Maxine Clarke

New and Classic Cocktails without Alcohol

First published by Stacey International 1989
128 Kensington Church Street, London W8 4BH
Telex: 298768 STACEY G
Fax: 01 792 9288

Set in Linotronic Goudy Old Style by SX Composing Ltd,
Essex, England.

Printed and bound by the Tien Wah Press, Singapore

ISBN 0 905743 54 7

British Library Cataloguing-in-Publication Data
Sutton, Robert
New and Classic Cocktails without Alcohol
1. Soft drinks – Recipes
I. Title   II. Pointing, Keith
641.8'75

CONTENTS

The authors would like to acknowledge the help,
supply of products, and loan of *objets d'art* from
the following:

Andrea (*recipe for 'Wild Horse'*); Pam Batty (*fine fabrics*); Winifred Bullen (*objets d'art*); Crosse & Blackwell (*Worcestershire sauce*); Jackie Dickens (*Egyptian silver bracelet*); Fatma (*recipe for 'Mayflower'*); Flower House, London W1 (*flowers*); Guinness (*Kaliber alcohol-free lager*); Celeste Henney (*cocktail equipment*); Joy Killaspy (*punch bowls*); Libby's (*fruit juices*); Lipton (*fine teas*); Vernon Morgan (*objets d'art*); John Nalty (*cocktail equipment*); Royal Brierley (*crystal*); Debbie Smith (*cocktail equipment*); Tom Stacey (*antique Arabian/Asian accoutrements and utensils*); Abdul-Ilah Tawfik (*antique Arabian/Asian accoutrements and utensils, and creative advice on Eastern drinks*); Pepsico (*suppliers of 7-Up*).

INTRODUCTION

To many people 'Cocktails' still means only one thing: a smart and sophisticated gathering at which complicated, beautiful and distinctly alcoholic drinks are served. But all this is changing; a quiet revolution is underway. For cocktails can be special without being expensive or fiddly or even exotic. And above all, they need not be alcoholic.

This book is dedicated to the millions of people worldwide who choose to eschew alcohol in their cocktails, whether for reasons of religion, or health, or just taste (for it is an oft-forgotten truth that alcohol deadens the palate). In the West this is a new and growing phenomenon, (as more and more people realise that drinking and working and drinking and driving simply do not go together), but in other parts of the world, the Middle East, for example, cocktails have long been non-alcoholic. Indeed it is possible that the basic concept of the cocktail, a mixture of flowers or fruits in water, was first invented in the Middle East.

As the title of this book suggests, some of the cocktails we include are tried and trusted favourites, while others are brand new recipes. Whether compiling or devising, we have drawn on the wonderful range of flavours, textures and colours that are available from fresh fruits and their juices, and from tea, coffee, milk and spices, as well as from such man-made delights as cola, 7-Up, tonic water and ginger ale.

Here you will find non-alcoholic cocktails of every shape and size. They may be visually elaborate art for formal occasions with lots of ingredients and preparation – but they needn't be. There are just as many that can be made in under a minute to liven up a hasty snack, provide a lift on a cold winter morning or quench your thirst on a blazing hot day.

Since there are cocktails for all occasions, we have grouped the recipes in this book by mood and occasion rather than by ingredients. Alongside you will find chapters on the more celebrated Eastern and Western cocktail classics, as well as many tips on how to present your cocktails with flair, and the equipment that will make it easier. A short glossary at the back of the book sheds light on the origins of the more mysterious cocktail names, and a separate glossary of illustrations identifies some of the more intriguing objects used in Vernon Morgan's photographs.

Freed from alcohol, cocktails are for any and for every day, and the 'Cocktail Hour' is as much eight in the morning or three in the afternoon as seven at night. And each time you partake of the inexhaustible variety that is on offer, you can – quite literally – drink to your own health.

Robert Sutton
Keith Pointing
London 1989

With the right equipment it is easier to make cocktails well. It can be more enjoyable too – an element of ritual adds to the sense of occasion that many cocktails demand. Some of the most useful pieces of cocktail-making equipment are illustrated here; ie a zester for removing zest from citrous fruits and a canelle knife which channels the peel.

If you are buying cocktail equipment, do choose it for its decorative as well as its practical qualities.

In addition, an electric blender and a good range of herbs and spices will greatly increase the variety of cocktails you can make.

1 3-piece standard cocktail shaker
2 Royal Brierley crystal jug
3 Royal Brierley crystal decanter
4 Swizzle stick
5 Corkscrew
6 Bottle stopper
7 Champagne cork extractor
8 Bottle opener
9 Zester
10 Canelle knife
11 Cigar cutters
12 Ice tongs
13 Cocktail spoon
14 Cocktail stirrer
15 Lipton tea
16 Ice bucket
17 Kaliber alcohol-free lager
18 7-Up
19 Crosse & Blackwell Worcestershire Sauce
20 Libby's juices
21 Nescafé

Cider glass   Coupe   Standard cocktail   Flute

Tankard   Double cocktail   Rocks   Wine glass

Goblet   Balloon   Thimble   Highball glass

MAKING COCKTAILS

The ingredient measurements used in this book are given in metric and its equivalent in US fluid measure. If you wish to use UK imperial measure please convert using the table below.

When working out the quantities you need to remember that a flute, coupe or standard cocktail glass holds around 120 ml (4 US fl oz); rocks or highball glasses hold around double that.

All the recipes in this book are intended to guide rather than direct: palates differ and you may wish to slightly alter the proportions of the main ingredients, and in particular to use more or less sugar, salt, or spices.

Unless specified, it is not essential to strain fresh juices, although it is preferable. This is best achieved by decanting or straining through muslin.

In some instances we have given brand names where specific products (such as Libby's fruit juices, Kaliber alcohol-free lager or Lipton tea) have produced especially satisfactory results. If you cannot obtain these particular brands, suitable alternatives can of course be used.

METRIC	USA	BRITISH
4.5 litres		1 gallon/8 pints
3.8 litres	1 gallon/8 pints	
1 litre (= 1000 mililitres)	2.11 pints	1.76 pints
¾ litre (= 750 ml)	1.58 pints	1.32 pints
568 ml	1.2 pints/19 fl oz	1 pint/20 fl oz
500 ml/½ litre	1.06 pints/17 fl oz	18 fl oz
473 ml	1 pint/16 fl oz	0.83 pint/18 fl oz
300 ml	0.6 pint/10 fl oz	11 fl oz
200 ml	6.5 fl oz	7 fl oz
100 ml	3 fl oz	3.5 fl oz
50 ml	1.5 fl oz	2 fl oz
30 ml	1 fl oz	
28 ml		1 fl oz
15 ml	1 tablespoon	1 tablespoon
5 ml	1 teaspoon	1 teaspoon
454 gm	1 pound (lb)	1 lb
100 gm	3 ounces (oz)	3 oz
30 gm	1 oz	1 oz

EASTERN CLASSICS

THERE IS A STRONG POSSIBILITY THAT
COCKTAILS WERE FIRST MADE IN THE EAST.
HERE IS A SELECTION OF SOME CLASSIC
DRINKS AND MORE UNUSUAL EASTERN
SHERBETS AND JULEPS.

GELUB (ROSEWATER)

200 gm/6 oz red/pink rose petals
100 gm/3 oz sugar
1 litre/2 pints water
juice of ½ lemon

This is the classic Middle Eastern cocktail from which the western 'julep' takes its name.

Wash the petals well and simmer them in water with sugar and the juice from half a lemon. Allow to cool. Pour onto ice in flutes decorated with a rose. Drink either straight or topped up with soda water.

The sugar quantities should be adjusted according to taste.

Serves 6-8

TYRE TEA

5 teaspoons aniseed
1 teaspoon ground cinnamon
1 litre/2 pints water
sugar to taste
chopped almonds and/or walnuts

Bring the water to the boil and add cinnamon and aniseed for 2-3 minutes. Strain and allow to cool. Pour into coupes or wine glasses. Add sugar to taste. Add chopped nuts to each glass.

If you can find star of anise (*see illustration*) then you may use these, having ground them first in a pestle and mortar.

Serves 4-8
ILLUSTRATED

TAMARIND JUICE

500 gm/1 lb tamarind pods
500 gm/1 lb sugar (or to taste)
1-1½ litres/2-3 pints of water

Soak thoroughly washed tamarind pods for 8-12 hours; alternatively you may be able to buy these ready prepared.

Chop and press the softened pods through a sieve, and discard the remains. Put the tarmarind juice into the water used for soaking, add sugar and bring to the boil, stirring and simmering whilst the sugar dissolves. Allow to cool. Dilute with iced water to taste.

Serve long in highball glasses or 'on the rocks' in rocks glasses.

Serves 6-8

TEE ARABE (HIBISCUS TEA)

100 gm/3 oz hibiscus flowers – preferably fresh
50 gm/1½ oz sugar
1 litre/2 pints water
soda water

Simmer the hibiscus and the sugar in the water for 5-8 minutes, and then allow the brew to cool. Pour onto ice in cider glasses or small tankards. Top up with soda water.

Decorate each glass with a hibiscus flower, if available.

Serves 5-8

MINT TEA JULEP

300 ml/10 fl oz freshly made Lipton tea
2 tablespoons Lipton honey (clear)
2 tablespoons lemon juice
4 mint leaves
ice cubes
soda water

Whilst the tea is still hot stir in the honey and
chill. Add lemon juice. Half fill the glasses with
ice and add a mint leaf to each. Pour in the tea
and top up with soda water.

Serves 4

WESTERN CLASSICS

MANY WESTERN NON-ALCOHOLIC
COCKTAILS DATE FROM THE 1920s AND '30s.
THIS IS A SELECTION OF SOME OF THE MORE
FAMOUS CONCOCTIONS OF THAT ERA.

ST. CLEMENTS
(ORANGES AND LEMONS)

500 ml/1 pint orange juice
500 ml/1 pint bitter lemon (or 50 ml/1.5 fl oz fresh lemon
  juice)

Pour the ingredients over ice in a mixing jug, stir well and serve in highball glasses decorated with slices of orange and lemon.

You can also frost glass rims with orange juice and caster sugar.

Serves 6

SHIRLEY TEMPLE

250 ml/8 fl oz passion fruit juice
300 ml/10 fl oz pineapple or lime juice
7-Up or soda water to top up

Blend the juice with ice in a blender until creamy, then pour into highball glasses. Top up with 7-Up or soda water.

Decorate with a cocktail stick of cubed fresh pineapple and cocktail straws.

For added colour place red (cochineal) coloured ice cubes in the glasses.

Serves 6

ILLUSTRATED

PUSSYFOOT

50 ml/1.5 fl oz lemon juice
50 ml/1.5 fl oz orange juice
50 ml/1.5 fl oz lime juice
1 dash grenadine
1 egg yolk or 15 ml/tablespoon cream
7-Up or soda water to top up

One of the more famous Western classics, available in many hotels and bars.

Shake (or blend) the ingredients with ice and serve in highball glasses. Top up with 7-Up or soda water. Cocktail straws, parasols and sticks of cherries or olives are *de rigueur* with this cocktail.

Serves 1

LIMEY

400 ml/14 fl oz lime juice
400 ml/14 fl oz lemon juice
1 egg white

Blend the ingredients with ice in a blender until
foamy and pour into cocktail glasses. Decorate
with a stick of green cocktail cherries and lime
slices. For those who prefer less astringency, caster
sugar may be added to taste during blending.

Serves 4-6

ILLUSTRATED

GRECIAN

200 ml/7 fl oz peach juice
100 ml/3 fl oz orange juice
50 ml/1.5 fl oz lemon juice
soda water to top up

Blend all the ingredients well with ice and pour
into a large goblet. Top up with soda water and
decorate with slices of orange, lemon and lime.

Serves 1-2

ROSY PIPPIN

1 dash grenadine
100 ml/3 fl oz apple juice
squeeze of lemon juice
American ginger ale to top up

Mix the ingredients with ice and pour into a large
wine glass. Top up with American ginger ale.
Decorate with slices of apple or cocktail sticks of
apple and stem ginger.

Serves 1

PARSON'S PARTICULAR

100 ml/3 fl oz orange juice
50 ml/1.5 fl oz lemon juice
1 egg yolk
4 dashes grenadine

Shake or blend the ingredients well with ice, then
strain into a cocktail glass. Serve decorated with a
cocktail cherry.

Serves 1

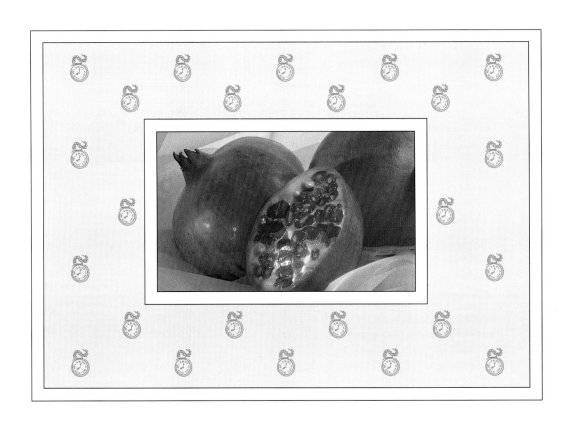

MINUTE MAKERS

THEIR SIMPLE INGREDIENTS ENSURE
THESE COCKTAILS CAN BE MADE
QUICKLY.

SUNSET

2 dashes grenadine or 10 ml/2 teaspoons pomegranate juice
ginger ale

Fill a coupe three-quarters full of ginger ale
and then add the grenadine or pomegranate
juice. Decorate with a cherry, or the fruit
of a pomegranate on a stick.

Serves 1

UGLI

150 ml/5 fl oz Libby's orange juice
150 ml/5 fl oz Libby's grapefruit juice

Take a highball glass of ice and pour in equal parts of Libby's orange and grapefruit juice. Pour into a mixing glass and then back into the highball glass.

Decorate with a slice of orange, an orange-coloured flower (eg nasturtium), cocktail straws and parasols.

Serves 1

ILLUSTRATED

APPLE ALE

250 ml/8 fl oz sparkling apple juice
250 ml/8 fl oz dry ginger ale

Thoroughly chill the ingredients. Mix together and serve in rocks glasses. Garnish with several red cherries and orange slices in the drink.

Serves 2-4

KOOL KOCKTAIL

200 ml/7 fl oz lemon juice
2 dashes grenadine or 10 ml/2 teaspoons pomegranate juice
1 egg yolk
sugar

Shake the ingredients well with ice and strain the mixture into cocktail glasses. Add sugar to taste. Decorate with a cherry on a stick.

Serves 2

TAIF TULIP

500 ml/1 pint tonic water (or lime Perrier)
fresh mint

Mix tonic water and crushed ice together and crush several sprigs of fresh mint into them.

Serve in tulip-fluted glasses and decorate with a mint leaf.

Serves 4

GINGERED ORANGE

1 part Libby's orange juice
1 part ginger ale

Fill a jug or large wine glass with ice and pour in equal parts of Libby's orange juice and ginger ale (dry or American) to taste.

Decorate with a slice of orange.

ILLUSTRATED

PUKKA CHUKKA

30 ml/1 fl oz lime juice
ginger beer

Half fill a highball glass with ice and add the lime juice and then top up with ginger beer. Stir well and decorate with a slice of fresh lime or lemon.

Serves 1

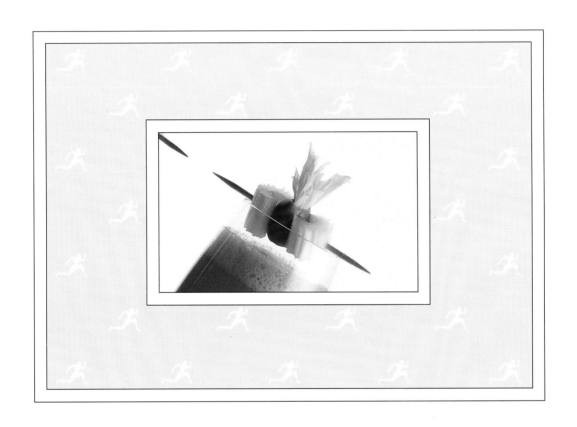

HI-HEALTH

THESE COCKTAILS ARE EITHER LOW IN SUGAR
AND CALORIES OR HIGH IN PROTEIN AND
VITAMINS.

ICED LEMON TEA

Lipton tea
lemon juice

Make Lipton or Lipton Earl Grey tea (not too strong), add lemon juice and either refrigerate or shake with ice cubes until cool. Garnish with a slice of lemon. Fresh mint leaves may be added for further flavour.

UP-BEET

350 ml/12 fl oz Libby's tomato juice
350 ml/12 fl oz beetroot juice
salt
pepper
Crosse & Blackwell Worcestershire sauce
squeeze of lemon/lime juice

Pour the two juices onto ice in a mixing jug. Add a squeeze of lemon or lime, salt, pepper and, if you want it spicy, Crosse & Blackwell Worcestershire sauce. Stir well and serve in cocktail or highball glasses. Decorate with cocktail sticks of celery and olives or celery and fresh mint.

Serves 4-6

ILLUSTRATED

JASPER

250 ml/8 fl oz carrot juice
250 ml/8 fl oz cranberry juice
squeeze of lemon juice
pinch of celery salt

Shake the two juices onto ice with a dash of lemon and a pinch of celery salt. Strain into highball glasses garnished with cocktail sticks of celery and carrot pieces.

Serves 3-4

LEAN MACHINE

250 ml/8 fl oz carrot juice
1 leaf of spinach
3 cubes of celery
1 sprig of parsley

Place all the ingredients in a blender and process thoroughly. Ideally, the carrot juice should be fresh: 1 lb/450 g of carrots will produce approximately ½ pint/250 ml of juice. If fresh carrots are used, the mixture should be strained. Then pour onto ice in highball glasses or tankards. Add a dash of Worcestershire sauce and a pinch of salt if you wish. Decorate with sticks of carrot and celery pieces.

Serves 1-2

SANTÉ

750 ml/1½ pints Libby's pineapple juice
250 ml/8 fl oz redcurrant juice
lime juice to taste

Shake ingredients with ice in a cocktail shaker. Serve in cocktail glasses decorated with cubes of pineapple and redcurrants.

Serves 6-8

SLIM JIM

250 ml/8 fl oz Libby's grapefruit juice
250 ml/8 fl oz Libby's tomato juice
Crosse & Blackwell Worcestershire sauce

Pour the Libby's juices onto ice in a cocktail
shaker and add dash(es) of Crosse & Blackwell
Worcestershire sauce and/or tabasco. Shake well
and strain into flutes or cocktail glasses. Garnish
with slivers of grapefruit skin placed in the glass or
with pieces of celery and cocktail olives on sticks.

Serves 4

ILLUSTRATED

TROPIC

120 ml/4 fl oz mango juice
250 ml/8 fl oz orange juice
300 ml/10 fl oz soda water or orange Perrier
squeeze of lemon juice
pinch of ground ginger
sugar (to taste)

Blend or shake fruit juices (fresh of possible)
thoroughly with ice, a pinch of ginger and sugar,
if you need it. Pour into a large jug and mix in
soda water. Serve in cider glasses or small tankards
decorated with a slice of orange or lime.

Serves 2-4

APPLEADE

½ teaspoon caster sugar
2 large eating apples
300 ml/10 fl oz boiling water

Dice the apples and pour the boiling water over them. Add the sugar and strain into a jug. Allow to cool, then pour into highball glasses half full of ice and serve. Decorate with a slice of apple.

Serves 2

SPORTSMAN

30 ml/1 fl oz lime cordial
30 ml/1 fl oz lemon juice
½ teaspoon rose-hip syrup (or grenadine)
tonic water to top up

Pour ingredients over ice cubes in a highball glass. Top up with tonic water. You may wish to add sugar if it is too dry.

Serves 1

RASPBERRY MILK

500 ml/1 pint milk (evaporated milk may also be used)
250-300 ml/8-10 fl oz raspberry juice (fresh raspberries if available)
sugar to taste

Mix thoroughly, preferably in a blender, with or without sugar. Pour into cocktail or cider glasses and decorate with cocktail sticks of fresh raspberries and mint leaves.

Serves 2-4

ILLUSTRATED

STRAWBERRY YOGHURT

500 ml/1 pint of liquid low fat yoghurt
250 gm/8 oz pureed strawberries
caster sugar (optional)

Add the caster sugar if you wish and then blend the ingredients together. Serve in coupe glasses decorated with slices of fresh strawberries.

Serves 3-4

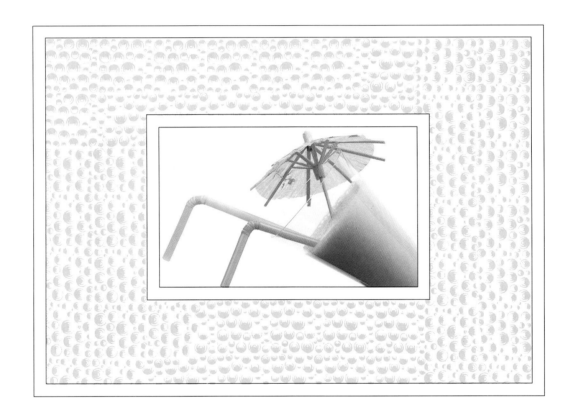

SHEER FUN

COCKTAILS ARE AS MUCH ABOUT FUN AND
AMUSEMENT AS ELEGANCE OR SLAKING THIRST.
THESE ARE PARTY-GOERS, YOUTHFULLY
EYE-CATCHING.

SUN GROVE

200 ml/7 fl oz orange juice
ginger syrup
7-Up (or squeeze of lime and soda water)

Pour the orange juice onto ice in a highball glass. Add
a dash of ginger syrup and top up with 7-Up (or lime
and soda water for a drier taste) and a spiral of orange
(or lime).

Serves 1

PEACH LASSI

1 part liquid yoghurt
1 part peach juice
1 part banana

Blend equal quantities of yoghurt, peach juice and banana. Serve in wine glasses with cocktail sticks of orange and banana.

ILLUSTRATED

HALVA CREAM

30 gm/1 oz sesame halva
350 ml/12 fl oz plain yoghurt
350 ml/12 fl oz milk

Blend the halva, yoghurt and milk in a blender with or without ice. Serve in glass tankards or coupes with cocktail sticks of raisins and sultanas.

Serves 2-5

APPLE MEG

500 ml/1 pint still apple juice
250 ml/½ pint vanilla ice cream
ground nutmeg
double cream

Blend the ice cream lightly before adding the apple juice and a teaspoon of nutmeg. Blend further.

Serve in coupe glases topped with double cream (preferably whipped) and dusted with nutmeg.

Serves 6-8

COCOLATE

250 ml/8 fl oz milk
Half a coconut (shredded)
100 gm/3 oz chocolate or carob (sugar-free chocolate substitute)
mint (optional)

Melt down the chocolate (or carob) and blend with the milk. Cool, add ice (and mint to taste) and serve in glass tankards. Decorate the surface of each tankard with shredded coconut.

Serves 1

POM POM

1 egg white
juice of 1 lemon
1 dash grenadine or pomegranate juice
7-Up or soda water to top up

May be shaken, but it is easier to put ice, lemon juice, grenadine and egg white in a blender. Then strain over crushed ice into a coupe glass. Top up with 7-Up or soda water.

Serves 1

ILLUSTRATED

GREEN SATIN

500 ml/1 pint milk
300 ml/10 fl oz vanilla ice cream
2 teaspoons sirop de menthe

Blend the ingredients thoroughly in a blender. Serve with green-coloured ice cubes in highball glasses. Dress the top of the drinks with a sprinkling of powdered chocolate and a small sprig of mint.

Serves 4

STRAWBERRY SHERBERT

250 gm/8 oz strawberries
250 gm/8 oz sugar
600 ml/20 fl oz water
crushed ice

Hull and chop the strawberries. Make a syrup by boiling the sugar and water. Cool. Put half the strawberries and half the syrup in a blender until foamy and smooth. Repeat using the remainder. Pour onto plenty of crushed ice in flat coupe glasses and decorate with whole strawberries and their leaves.

Serves 6-8

SLOW MORNINGS

IF YOU OR THE MORNING ARE SLOW OR BLUE,
ENLIVEN YOUR DAY WITH ONE OF THESE
SPARKLING COCKTAILS.

SHARP START

250 ml/8 fl oz non-alcoholic white wine
100 ml/3 fl oz dry ginger ale or ginger beer
100 ml/3 fl oz tonic water
pinch of ground ginger or dash of ginger syrup
pinch of cayenne pepper or dash of tabasco

Pour the ingredients into a mixing jug and stir
gently with ice. Serve in cocktail glasses decorated
with olives and a lemon twist, or with halved
grapes and pieces of stem ginger. Frost glass rims
lightly with fine salt and, for added colour, with
blue edible colouring.

Serves 2-3

CLAMATOE

250 ml/8 fl oz Libby's tomato juice
250 ml/8 fl oz clam juice

Pour the juices onto ice in a shaker and add a
squeeze of lemon, and salt and black pepper to
taste. Shake well and strain into cocktail glasses.
Garnish with a lemon slice or cocktail sticks of
olives and split baby tomatoes.

Serves 2-4

ILLUSTRATED

KANDARA FIZZ

orange juice
non-alcoholic sparkling white wine

Fill a highball glass with crushed ice. Quarter fill
with orange juice, then add the non-alcoholic
sparkling white wine and garnish with a slice of
orange.

Serves 1

FIRST AID

juice of 2 lemons
2 teaspoons blackcurrant syrup
½ teaspoon sugar
soda water to top up

Mix in a tumbler with crushed ice. Add a slice of
lemon and top up with soda water.

Serves 1

THE CARTLAND CURE

1 egg
1 banana
2 dessertspoons yoghurt
1 teaspoon Lipton honey
1 teaspoon wheatgerm
1 teaspoon lecithin
40 ml/1.5 fl oz evaporated milk

Place all the ingredients in a blender and blend
until smooth. Pour into a large goblet or highball
glass and sprinkle the top with crushed hazelnuts.

Serves 1

SUNRISE

250 gm/8 oz cooked baby carrots, diced
450 ml/15 fl oz Libby's orange juice
150 ml/5 fl oz chicken or herb stock
8 dashes tabasco sauce
2 egg whites
ice cubes

Put the carrots, Libby's orange juice, stock and tabasco, with one egg white and ice into a blender and process until smooth. Whisk the remaining egg white until stiff. Pour the cocktail into fluted glasses, then add a froth of egg white to each.

Decorate with slices of kiwi fruit.

Serves 6-8

CAIRENE

250 ml/8 fl oz Libby's tomato juice
juice of 1 lemon
pinch of salt
pepper
1 dash Crosse & Blackwell Worcestershire sauce
1 dash tabasco

Half fill a large goblet with ice and add the ingredients. Pour into a mixing glass and back into the goblet. Repeat this twice. Decorate with a slice of lemon and a fanned stick of celery.

Serves 1

ILLUSTRATED

SAHARA STING

250 ml/8 fl oz ginger beer
2 dashes bitters
1 dash lime juice

Mix the ingredients with ice and pour into a glass tankard. Decorate with a slice of fresh lime.

Serves 1

EGG NOG

300 ml/10 fl oz milk or single cream
1 egg
caster sugar to taste

Blend the ingredients with or without ice in a blender until smooth. Pour into coupes and then dust with nutmeg or chocolate.

May be served cold, at room temperature or warmed.

Serves 2-3

ARID DAYS

WHEN IT IS 95 DEGREES IN THE SHADE, KEEP COOL
WITH ONE OF THESE THIRST-QUENCHERS.

HELIOPOLE

700 ml/1½ pints still or sparkling non-alcoholic wine (white
  preferably) or apple juice
mint leaves
squeeze of lime juice
cardamom

Pour the non-alcoholic white wine or apple juice
into a mixing jug with ice. Add one or two
squeezes of lime or a little lime cordial, and stir
well. Strain into highball glasses and add mint
leaves or a pinch of crushed cardamom.

Decorate with a twirl of lemon or lime peel.

Serves 3-4

SHANDY

1 bottle Kaliber alcohol-free lager
1 bottle or can 7-Up

Mix the iced non-alcoholic lager with iced 7-Up. Serve with a slice of lemon, in goblets or tankards.

Serves 2

ILLUSTRATED

LAGER AND LIME

1 bottle Kaliber alcohol-free lager
1 dash lime cordial or a squeezed wedge of fresh lime

Serve the iced non-alcoholic lager and lime in a goblet or tankard. Decorate with a slice of lemon or lime.

(An English favourite and now increasingly popular in North America.)

ZIPP

1 bottle Kaliber alcohol-free lager
1 bottle (350 ml/12 fl oz) Pepsi-Cola
squeeze of lemon juice
squeeze of orange juice

Mix the iced Pepsi-Cola and non-alcoholic lager together and squeeze in some lemon and orange juice. Serve with a slice of orange in goblets or tankards.

Serves 2-4

ICED COFFEE

4 dessertspoons Nescafé instant coffee
6 dessertspoons sugar (or to taste)
fresh milk

Put the coffee and sugar into a 1 litre/2 pint coffee pot or jug, add a small amount of boiling water and stir until dissolved. Fill the pot with cold water and chill in the refrigerator. Quarter-fill cider or rocks glasses with black iced coffee. Top up with cold milk and add an ice cube. Garnish with whipped cream.

A quicker way of preparing this is to mix the Nescafé with milk and sugar and then blend it with ice in a blender.

Serves 6

ILLUSTRATED

GREEN SPIKE

350 ml/12 fl oz tonic water
10 ml/2 teaspoons sirop de menthe

Stir the ingredients in a mixing jug or in a glass with ice. Pour into double cocktail glasses frosted with caster sugar and sirop de menthe.

Decorate with fresh mint leaves and/or cocktail sticks of diced apple and olives.

Serves 2

JEDDAH JEWEL

500 ml/1 pint Libby's orange juice
100 ml/3 fl oz lemon or lime juice
bitters
7-Up or soda water to top up
sirop de framboise or raspberry juice

Mix the juices and 2-5 dashes of bitters well with ice, pour into straight-sided goblets or highball glasses and top up with 7-Up or soda. Decorate with twirls or slices of orange and lemon. Drift sirop de framboise through the drink.

Serves 4-6

ILLUSTRATED

COOL CUCUMBER

300 ml/10 fl oz liquid natural yoghurt
¼ cucumber
7-Up or soda water to top up
squeeze of lime juice
salt

Skin the cucumber and remove the seeds, then blend it with the yoghurt, a squeeze of lime juice and a pinch of salt. Pour onto ice in rocks glasses, filling them half to two-thirds full. Top up with 7-Up or soda water. Decorate with cocktail sticks of cubed cucumber and fresh mint leaves.

Serves 2

DAMASCUS DAMSEL

1-1½ kg/2-3 lb watermelon
1 orange
½ lemon
ground ginger
250 ml/8 fl oz soda water

Peel and deseed the fruit and cut them into pieces. Blend together, adding a dash of ground ginger. Strain. Stir in the soda water onto ice cubes in a mixing jug or punch bowl. Serve in cocktail glasses or tankards with rims frosted with sugar. Decorate with a slice of orange on the edge of each glass.

Serves 4-6

STRAWBERRY PUNCH

1 litre/2 pints pineapple juice
juice from 6 lemons
2 bottles sparkling white grape juice
700 gm/1½ lb sieved fresh strawberries

Pour the pineapple and lemon juice into a glass or silver punch bowl and add plenty of ice. Then add the hulled and cut strawberries and the grape juice. Serve in glass tankards or large goblets decorated with strawberries.

Serves 12-18

DESERT FLOWER

1 litre/2 pints soda water
200 gm/6 oz stem ginger
cardamom
salt (or sugar)

Prior to making this cocktail soak the stem ginger overnight in ½ litre/1 pint of soda water with two or three cloves of ground cardamom. Decant the mixture into flutes or coupes leaving the sediment behind and top up with soda water, coloured with edible colouring if you wish. Cocktail sticks of olives (with a salt frost) or red cocktail cherries (with a sugar frost) can also be used.

Serves 6-8

ILLUSTRATED

SPRING FANCY

10 ml/2 teaspoons cassis (blackcurrant)
1 dash lemon juice
7-Up or soda water

Fill a highball glass with ice, then pour in the 7-Up until the glass is three-quarters full. Add the lemon juice, and the cassis (which will float to the top). Decorate with a slice of lemon and cocktail straws.

Serves 1

CIDER ICE

200 ml/7 fl oz vanilla ice cream
400 ml/14 fl oz non-alcoholic still cider
ground nutmeg
whipped cream

Lightly blend the ice cream until soft, then add the non-alcoholic cider and several pinches of nutmeg. Blend further until frothy. Decorate with whipped cream and sprinkle with nutmeg.

Serves 4

GREY DAYS

IF IT'S GREY AND OVERCAST, OR CHILLY, THESE
COCKTAILS WILL WARM AND CONSOLE. SOME
MAY BE SERVED HOT, OTHERS ARE SPICY.

BEAR HUG

400 gm/12 oz evaporated milk or single cream
2 tablespoons Lipton honey (clear)
juice of 2 oranges
cardamom/ginger/nutmeg/cinnamon

Add a pinch of cardamom and/or ginger, nutmeg
and cinnamon and 2 tablespoons of clear honey to
the evaporated milk and stir thoroughly; then add
the juice. Serve in rocks or tumblers with slices of
orange, dust with nutmeg and ginger.

Serves 2-4

MULLED APPLE JUICE

1 litre/2 pints still apple juice (or non-alcoholic cider)
6 cloves
nutmeg
1 stick of cinnamon
2 tablespoons demerara sugar
pinch of ground ginger
rind of 1 orange and 1 lemon

Slowly mull or simmer the ingredients in a
stainless steel saucepan for about 45 minutes.
Serve hot, decanting into glass tankards or
goblets, decorated with half slices of lemon and/or
orange. May also be served chilled. Decorate with
skins of orange or twirls of orange rind floating in
glasses, or (*see illustration*) with sticks of apple
stuck with cloves floating in the glasses.

Non-alcoholic red wine may also be mulled in the
same way.

Serves 4-6

ILLUSTRATED

DOT'S HOT SPOT

250 ml/8 fl oz non-alcoholic white wine
250 ml/8 fl oz apple juice
half stick of cinnamon
2 tablespoons Lipton honey (clear)

Heat the ingredients in a saucepan for 4-5
minutes. Allow to cool slightly, strain and pour
onto ice in a glass. Decorate with a slice of lemon
floating on top of the drink.

Serves 2

DESERT PEARL

200 ml/7 fl oz tomato juice
1 egg yolk
2 dashes wine vinegar
pepper
1 teaspoon Crosse & Blackwell Worcestershire sauce
1 dash tabasco

Place ingredients, minus the egg yolk, in a wine
glass and stir thoroughly. Add the yolk on top,
taking care not to break it.

Serves 1

PINEAPPLE AND GINGER POLL

1 large ripe pineapple
250 gm/8 oz sugar
600 ml/20 fl oz water
juice of 2 lemons
2 tablespoons preserved ginger syrup

Remove the leafy top from the pineapple and put
it to one side. Cube the pineapple, discarding the
skin. Reserve one-third of the cubed fruit and
place it in a serving jug. Make a syrup by boiling
sugar and water. Cool. Add the lemon juice and
ginger syrup. Put two-thirds of the pineapple cubes
and the syrup in a blender and process. Half fill
the jug with ice and add the liquid from the
blender. Decorate the jug with the pineapple top.

Serves 8

ILLUSTRATED

JERSEY LILLY

250 ml/8 fl oz sparkling non-alcoholic cider
1 dash bitters
¼ teaspoon sugar

Stir the ingredients with ice in a mixing glass and
strain into a wine glass. Decorate with a cocktail
cherry.

Serves 1

RUWI SHRUB

300 ml/10 fl oz cherry juice
200 ml/7 fl oz passion fruit juice
bitters to taste

Shake the cherry and passion fruit juices in a
cocktail shaker with ice. Add the bitters and serve
in coupes. Decorate the rims of the glasses with
fresh, stoned cherries or sticks of cocktail cherries.

Serves 4-6

TROPICAL FRUIT YOGHURT

½ litre/1 pint liquid low fat yoghurt
250 gm/8 oz mango, guava and passion fruit purée
caster sugar (optional)

Simply blend the yoghurt and fruit purée together,
adding caster sugar to taste if required. Serve in
coupe glasses and decorate with slices of kiwi fruit
and grapes.

This cocktail can either be drunk or eaten with a
spoon.

Serves 4-6

WILD HORSE

400 ml/14 fl oz consommé
several squeezes of lemon juice
1 dash tabasco
1 dash Crosse & Blackwell Worcestershire sauce
pinch of salt

Half fill a large wine glass with ice and then add
all the ingredients. Pour from the glass into the
mixing glass and back again; repeat this twice.

Decorate with a stick of celery.

Serves 2-3

CHOCNUT

100 gm/3 oz chocolate or carob (sugar-free chocolate
  substitute)
200 gm/6 oz walnuts or hazelnuts
(150 gm/5 oz hazelnut chocolate/carob)
250 ml/8 fl oz milk

Melt down the chocolate or carob and blend with
the milk. Add ice and mint to taste and serve in
glass tankards. Decorate the surface of each
tankard with nut chips.

Serves 1

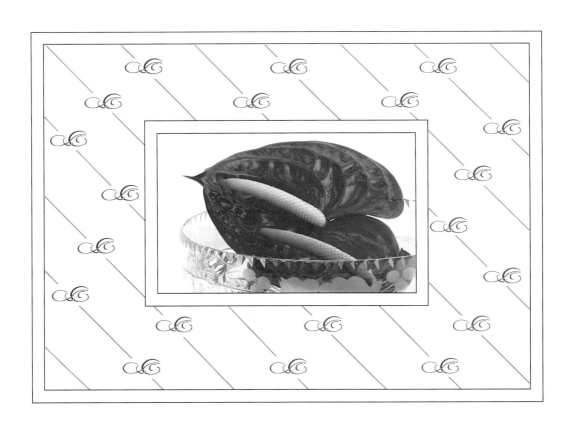

PRE-PRANDIAL

A SELECTION OF COCKTAILS THAT ARE GREAT BEFORE DINNER.

RED AXE

1 part Libby's tomato juice
1 part Kaliber alcohol-free lager

The ingredients should be very cold. Pour the tomato juice into a rocks glass and top up with an equal quantity of non-alcoholic lager. Decorate with olives and celery.

TONGA

40 ml/1.5 fl oz Libby's pineapple juice
juice of 1 lemon (or less to taste)
white of 1 egg
1 teaspoon grenadine syrup
7-Up to top up

Shake with ice. Strain into a highball glass with ice cubes. Top up with chilled 7-Up. Add pineapple cubes and kiwi fruit on sticks.

Serves 1

ILLUSTRATED

PINACOLADA

1 part pineapple juice
1 part coconut milk

Mix equal parts of pineapple juice and coconut milk with ice. This may be flavoured with a dash of blackcurrant, pomegranate or raspberry juice. Serve in coupes or highball glasses. Decorate with sticks of cocktail cherries and/or pineapple cubes.

KIR-DA

1 bottle sparkling non-alcoholic cider or sparkling non-
  alcoholic white wine
30 ml/1 fl oz cassis (blackcurrant) syrup
juice of 2 limes

Pour the ingredients onto ice in a mixing jug or punch bowl and stir gently. Serve in flutes; the rims may be frosted with juice and caster sugar.

Serves 6

RED SILK

250 ml/8 fl oz mulberry juice (freshly squeezed through
  muslin, if possible)
500 ml/1 pint non-alcoholic sparkling white wine
15 ml/1 tablespoon lime juice
60 gm/2 oz caster sugar

Stir sugar and lemon juice into mulberry juice, add to white wine and ice in a punch bowl. Float white rose petals in the bowl and ladle into flutes.

Serves 6

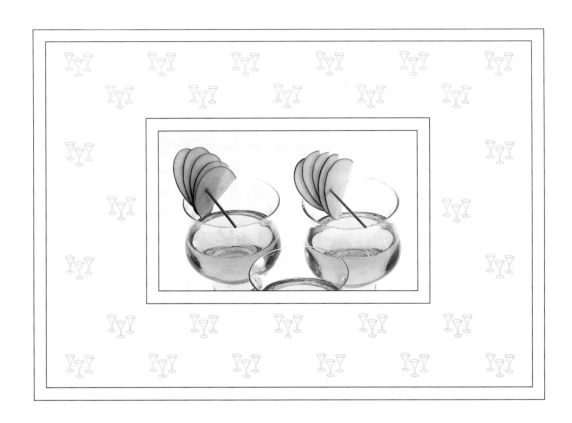

GATHERINGS

THESE FINELY BLENDED DRINKS COME INTO THEIR OWN AT
PARTIES, GARDEN RECEPTIONS AND OTHER FESTIVITIES.

SUMMER-SET

1 litre/2 pints non-alcoholic cider, sparkling or still
1 litre/2 pints dry ginger ale
juice of 1 lemon
juice of 1 lime
ginger syrup
cinnamon

Pour the non-alcoholic cider and dry ginger ale onto ice in a mixing jug or punch bowl. Add several dashes or ginger syrup, the lemon and lime juice and a pinch of cinnamon. Pour into wine glasses and decorate with a twist of lime and slices of apple.

Serves 10-12

PURPLE HAZE

750 ml/1½ pints non-alcoholic white wine, sparkling or still
50 ml/1.5 fl oz cassis syrup
25 ml/1 fl oz non-alcoholic pastis
7-Up or soda water

Stir wine, cassis and pastis with ice in a large jug. Strain into cider or cocktail glasses and add 7-Up or soda water.

Garnish with spliced grapes and fresh mint.

Serves 4-6

ILLUSTRATED

APPLE SHRUB

350 ml/12 fl oz sparkling non-alcoholic cider
350 ml/12 fl oz dry ginger ale

Pour the ingredients into a mixing jug with ice and stir gently. Serve in glass tankards or flutes and decorate with cubes of fresh apple and/or orange slices.

Serves 3-4

KNIGHT'S FIZZ

2-4 bottles of Kaliber alcohol-free lager
juice of 4 oranges
salt (or sugar)

Serve this cocktail in half-pint or in fluted glasses. Mix 2-4 bottles of non-alcoholic lager, the strained juice of 4 oranges and plenty of ice cubes into a jug. Decorate the edges of the glasses with frosted salt or sugar, and orange slices. This may be deliciously varied by using 250 ml/8 fl oz of gooseberry juice in place of the orange juice.

Serves 3-6

DURBAH PUNCH

400 ml/14 fl oz Lipton tea
cardamom
ground ginger
1 stick of cinnamon
juice of 2 oranges
juice of 1 lime
50 ml/1.5 fl oz redcurrant juice
soda water
sugar (optional)

Brew a pot of Lipton tea (2 teaspoons of tea or 1 tea bag) for two minutes. Strain off into a mixing jug, and while the tea is still hot add 3 opened cloves of cardamom, a stick of cinnamon, a pinch of ginger and (optional) 6 teaspoons of sugar. Stir and allow to cool. Then mix in the orange and lime juice. Add the redcurrant juice. Pour into a punch bowl, with plenty of ice. Top up with an equal quantity of soda water.

Decorate the punch bowl with slices of orange and fresh cherries. Serve in tumblers or rocks glasses with cocktail sticks of olives and diced celery or sliced kiwi fruit and oranges.

This cocktail can also be served warm.

Serves 8-12

ILLUSTRATED

SOUTHERN BELLE

sprig of mint
1 teaspoon caster sugar
squeeze of lemon juice
dry ginger ale to top up

Crush the mint and sugar in a mixing glass until the mint is pulverised, then add a dash of lemon juice. Pour into a tall glass full of ice and top up with the dry ginger ale. Decorate with fresh mint.

Serves 1

BUTTERFLY

1 litre/2 pints tonic water
1 can Pepsi-Cola
ginger
nutmeg
cinnamon
sugar

Take a large jug or punch bowl, put into it a
pinch of ginger, nutmeg and cinnamon and add
the Pepsi. Add a handful of ice and 6 lumps of
sugar and top up with tonic water. Stir well,
preferably with a silver cocktail spoon, and serve
onto ice. Decorate the jug and glasses with slices
of lemon or orange.

Serves 6-8

ILLUSTRATED

SOIRÉE

250 ml/½ pint non-alcoholic red wine
500 ml/1 pint dry ginger ale
500 ml/1 pint sparkling non-alcoholic white wine or cider

Pour all the ingredients into a punch bowl with
plenty of ice. Decorate the punch bowl with
spliced white and red grapes (and slivers of stem
ginger to taste). Serve in cocktail glasses or flutes.

Serves 10

GINGER AND IT

200 ml/7 fl oz non-alcoholic vermouth
100 ml/3 fl oz orange juice
500 ml/1 pint dry ginger ale

Pour the ingredients onto ice in a mixing glass.
Stir thoroughly. Serve in cocktail glasses with
sticks of cocktail cherries.

Serves 6-8

COCA SANA

300 ml/10 fl oz fresh coconut milk
300 ml/10 fl oz lime juice
1 litre/2 pints 7-Up

Shake the coconut milk and lime juice together in
a cocktail shaker. Mix in a punch bowl or a large
jug with 7-Up. Decorate with slices of lime or
cucumber. Serve in straight-sided goblets.

Serves 6-8

INDIAN APPLE

400 ml/14 fl oz cool unsweetened Lipton tea
400 ml/14 fl oz apple juice
400 ml/14 fl oz 7-Up or soda water
1 dash cranberry juice

Put plenty of ice in a mixing jug and pour in the
tea, apple juice and cranberry juice. Mix and top
up with 7-Up or soda water. Serve in glass
tankards and decorate with slices of apple
and mint.

Serves 4-5

APPLE SNOW

1 litre/2 pints non-alcoholic cider
juice of 8 oranges
juice of 2 lemons
4 egg whites
sugar to taste

Use a blender to blend all the ingredients with
ice. Pour into coupes and decorate with cubes of
apple and slices of orange on cocktail sticks.

Serves 6-8

CARDINAL PUNCH

500 ml/1 pint cranberry juice
100 ml/3 fl oz orange juice
50 ml/1.5 fl oz lemon juice
500 ml/1 pint ginger ale to top up

This cocktail is at its most eye-catching when prepared and served in a large glass or silver punch bowl with slices of orange and lemon and preferably fresh cranberries floating in it. Pour in all the juices onto ice and then top up with ginger ale. Serve with a ladle into decorated flute glasses.

Serves 7-10

ILLUSTRATED

EARL GREY'S APPLE PUNCH

600 ml/20 fl oz freshly-made Lipton Earl Grey Tea
10 cloves
600 ml/20 fl oz clear apple juice
600 ml/20 fl oz ginger ale
1 apple
3 tablespoons sugar

Make a pot of tea. Strain it onto the cloves while still hot, stirring in sugar until it dissolves. Then chill. Quarter-fill a large serving jug or pitcher with ice cubes and pour in the chilled tea (first removing the cloves). Add the apple juice and top up with the ginger ale. Decorate with a curl of apple peel and slices of apple. Serve in goblets or small tankards.

Serves 6-10

BRIGHT SPARK

200 ml/7 fl oz cranberry juice
400 ml/14 fl oz apple juice
squeeze of lime juice
bitters

Prepare the juices in a cocktail shaker with ice, a squeeze of lime and a few dashes of bitters. Strain into cocktail glasses and serve with sticks of olives.

Serves 4

ELEGANCE

THESE STYLISH COCKTAILS WILL TURN ANY
EVENING INTO AN OCCASION.

CHAMP BLEU

1 bottle sparkling non-alcoholic white wine (dry or sweet)
blue edible colouring

Chill the wine thoroughly. Serve in fluted glasses
and add a drop or so of colouring to produce the
depth of blue desired.

This is an eye-catching, even startling, cocktail.
Champ Vert (using a green edible colouring) is an
equally unusual alternative.

Serves 6

COFFEE DIGESTIF

300 ml/10 fl oz hot strong black Nescafé instant coffee
2 sticks cinnamon
2 tablespoons sugar
ice cubes
whipped double cream
4 pinches mixed spice
fresh cherries

Add the cinnamon sticks and sugar to the hot coffee (for convenience use Nescafé). Stir, and allow to cool. Pour over ice cubes. Serve in cocktail glasses, topped off with spoonfuls of cream and mixed spice. Decorate with cherries.

Serves 4

ILLUSTRATED

ARABIAN NIGHT

½ litre/1 pint non-alcoholic red wine
170 gm/6 oz tin of evaporated milk or single cream
6 teaspoons caster sugar

Stir 6 teaspoons of caster sugar into half a litre of non-alcoholic iced red wine; pour into cider glasses and pour milk or cream through the juice so that it forms a cascade.

Serves 4-6

PASSION GLOW

250 ml/8 fl oz passion fruit juice
250 ml/8 fl oz cherry juice
juice of 2 lemons
sugar to taste

Shake the ingredients well with ice in a
cocktail shaker. Strain into cocktail glasses
with rims frosted with cherry juice and caster
sugar. Decorate with a stick of fresh or
cocktail cherries.

Serves 4

SNAKE CHARMER

350 ml/12 fl oz Kaliber alcohol-free lager
100 ml/3 fl oz beetroot juice
100 ml/3 fl oz cranberry juice
a pinch of ground ginger and cardamom (to taste)

Stir the ingredients with ice in a mixing jug –
with or without spices to your taste. Serve in small
tankards or goblets, decorated with cocktail sticks
of cucumber and celery (or olives).

This cocktail is thirst quenching as well as
stimulating. Some people like a tiny pinch of salt
and pepper with it.

Serves 2-4

PINK BERLINER

30 ml/1 fl oz raspberry juice
1 bottle Kaliber alcohol-free lager

Put the ice into a glass tankard and pour in the
non-alcoholic lager. Add 30 ml/1 fl oz of raspberry
juice.

Serves 1

GRANDE DAME

200 ml/7 fl oz non-alcoholic red wine
100 ml/3 fl oz tonic water
2 squeezes of lemon juice

Shake the red wine and the lemon juice with ice
in a cocktail shaker. Decant into cocktail glasses.
Top up with tonic water. Decorate with a twist of
lemon.

Serves 2

ILLUSTRATED

GREEN BRIAR

juice of 6 lemons
dashes of sirop de menthe to taste
caster sugar to taste

Put the ingredients in a shaker with ice and shake
well. Strain into coupes or flutes. Decorate with
cocktail sticks of apple cubes and small mint
leaves, and sugar-frosted glasses.

For a longer drink, top up with lemon Perrier and
serve in flutes.

Serves 2

STRAWBERRY ROYALE

strawberry syrup
1 bottle sparkling non-alcoholic white wine

Pour a dash of strawberry syrup (preferably made by blending fresh strawberries) into each glass and add very cold sparkling white wine. Decorate with fresh strawberries and serve in coupes or flutes.

Serves 6

ILLUSTRATED

VERTU

300 ml/10 fl oz non-alcoholic vermouth
cassis syrup to taste
7-Up to top up

Shake the non-alcoholic vermouth and a dash of cassis with ice in a cocktail shaker. Pour into cocktail glasses, filling them one-third to one-half, and top them up with 7-Up.

Serves 2

PURPLE ORCHID

500 ml/1 pint blackcurrant juice
demerara sugar
ground cardamom
tonic water to top up
lemon

Pour the blackcurrant juice onto ice in a mixing jug. Stir in demerara sugar; top up with tonic water and add a squeeze of lemon. Decorate the mixing jug with a purple orchid; rub the glass rims with lemon rind and dip in caster sugar coloured with purple edible dye.

Serves 6-8

MAYFLOWER

1 litre/2 pints 7-Up
250 ml/½ pint non-alcoholic red wine
juice of 2 lemons
cinnamon
ground ginger
salt

Take a large glass or silver punch bowl and put in
2 or 3 handfuls of ice. Pour in the non-alcoholic
red wine, add a little ginger and cinnamon, and a
pinch of salt and the juice of two lemons; then
add the 7-Up. Prepare cocktail sticks of cocktail
cherries and cucumber and decorate the edge of
the glasses with slices of lemon. Serve in cider
glasses.

Serves 6-8

PRINCESS MARGRETE

5 large strawberries
1 large pineapple
juice of ½ lemon
juice of ½ orange
2 dashes strawberry juice

Place the chopped pineapple and other ingredients
in a blender with ice cubes and blend until
smooth. Pour into highball glasses and decorate
with a strawberry on the side of the glass. Frost
the edges of the glass with strawberry juice and
caster sugar.

Serves 2-4

ACAPULCO

400 ml/14 fl oz pineapple juice
200 ml/7 fl oz grapefruit juice
200 ml/7 fl oz single cream
caster sugar (to taste)

Mix the ingredients in a blender with ice. Serve
in straight-sided wine glasses, with cocktail straws
and sticks of cubed fresh pineapple and crisp
apple.

Serves 6-8

ILLUSTRATED

CAPUCINE

15 ml/1 tablespoon peppermint cordial
100 ml/3 fl oz cream or evaporated milk

Shake the ingredients with ice and then strain
into a coupe. Top up with crushed ice and
sprinkle with finely grated chocolate.

Serves 1

SAN FRANCISCO

150 ml/5 fl oz orange juice
150 ml/5 fl oz lemon juice
150 ml/5 fl oz pineapple juice
150 ml/5 fl oz grapefruit juice
2 dashes grenadine
1 egg white

Shake well (or blend) the ingredients with ice and
pour them into a large wine glass. Top up with
soda and decorate with slices of orange, lemon,
lime and pineapple speared with a cherry on a
stick, cocktail straws and parasols.

Serves 2-3

ONE THOUSAND AND ONE NIGHTS

100 ml/3 fl oz grenadine
500 ml/1 pint redcurrant juice (or pomegranate juice/syrup or
  cranberry juice)
500 ml/1 pint dry ginger ale
500 ml/1 pint tonic water
100 ml/3 fl oz cold black Nescafé instant coffee
100 ml/3 fl oz Pepsi-Cola
juice of 4 lemons
juice of 2 oranges
1 apple
bitters
orange bitters
stem ginger in syrup
cardamom
sugar

Pour the grenadine, ginger ale, redcurrant juice and tonic water into a large punch bowl or cocktail mixer jug; then add ice, black coffee, Pepsi and orange juice. Slice the apple and put it in with several dashes of bitters and orange bitters. Stir in the ground cardamom and 2 or 3 dessertspoons of sugar. Allow to stand in a refrigerator for at least 1-2 hours and then decant liquid or filter through cotton or muslin. Pour into goblets or tankards and decorate with cocktail sticks of stem ginger and fresh dates (or olives and diced apple).

Serves 6-10

CAIRENE	The adjective from Cairo.
CARTLAND	Named after Barbara Cartland, well-known British author of romantic fiction.
COCKTAIL	The origins of the word are obscure. One story, probably apocryphal, tells how the beautiful daughter of an Aztec king, Axolotel VIII, invented a drink so delicious that it helped the king resolve a long-standing quarrel with an old adversary.
	The Princess's name was Coctel, and thus the name for the new drink became 'cocktail'.
DURBAH	A court held by an Indian Prince. A formal reception marked by pledges of fealty given by his subjects to the prince or to an Anglo-Indian governor or viceroy.
EARL GREY	Earl Grey tea is named after the second Earl, Charles (1764-1845), who was Prime Minister of Great Britain, 1830-34.
HALVA	A Middle-Eastern flaky confection of crushed sesame seeds in a base of syrup (or honey).
JASPER	Semi-precious stone of hues ranging between green and red.
JULEP/GELUB	Julep is the cognate of *gelub* – the Arabic word for rosewater.
KANDARA	A major region of the city of Jeddah in Saudi Arabia.
KIR-DAR	Named after a French church dignitary called Kir, who also gave his name to the drink 'Kir'.
LIMEY	In the nineteenth century, English sailors were given fresh limes to prevent scurvy (lime juice is high in vitamin C). Hence 'Limey' became slang for an Englishman.
POLL	An eighteenth-century expression for a head, or, by extension, a wig. It is from this origin that terms such as election poll and poll tax are derived. In this cocktail the 'poll' is the head of a pineapple.
PUKKA CHUKKA	Both words originally came from Hindi. 'Pukka' now means genuine, authentic, or first-class; 'chukka' now means a polo-playing period in the equestrian game of polo.
PUSSYFOOT	A colloquial English expression, meaning to tread or move warily.
ROSY PIPPIN	A classic variety of English apple – yellow/green, flushed with red.
RUWI	A city in Oman.
ST CLEMENTS (Oranges & Lemons)	Named after the children's song, which is based on the bell peals of Christopher Wren's London churches: 'Oranges and lemons say the bells of St Clements. You owe me five farthings say the bells of St Martins. . . .'
SLIM JIM	A narrow striped tie fashionable in England in the 1950s.

SHRUB/SHERBET/ SORBET/SYRUP	Shrub and sherbet are drinks of fruit juice in water; sorbet is fruit juice ice. All four words have a common Arabic/Persian root meaning a drink.
TAIF	A beautiful ancient town in the western mountains of Saudi Arabia.
TONGA	A group of islands in the south-west Pacific.
TYRE	An ancient city in Lebanon.
UGLI	A natural fruit. Like the cocktail named after it, it is a cross between a grapefruit and an orange.

PICTORIAL GLOSSARY

Royal Brierley crystal has been used extensively in the photographs in this book. Individual pieces are identified below.

ACAPULCO	'Brain' coral; natural sponge; *Dracaena* foliage.
BUTTERFLY	*Alstroemeria* (Peruvian Lily).
CAIRENE	Egyptian silver bracelet, c.1890.
CHAMP BLEU	Fanned silver swizzle stick; Mahgrebian bone and silver bracelet c.1920; *Rosa* 'Medallion'.
COFFEE DIGESTIF	Tobacco water-pipe or 'hookah', Saudi Arabian c.1960.
DESERT FLOWER	*Schlumbergera truncata* (Christmas Cactus).
DURBAH PUNCH	Silver punch bowl; oriental Samovar.
GINGERED ORANGE	Spray Chrysanthemum.
ICED COFFEE	'Rose of the Desert' (crystalline rock from the Sahara); Arabian coffee pot; *Nigella* (dried Love-in-a-Mist).
JEDDAH JEWEL	Coral necklace; sapphire and opals; *Lilium* 'Connecticut King'.
LEADING LADY	Asprey cocktail glass.
MINT JULEP TEA	Omani *bisht* or cloak; Mahgrebian silver spoon.
MULLED APPLE JUICE	*Pyracantha*.
ONE THOUSAND & ONE NIGHTS	Camel saddlebag, Saudi Arabian, contemporary; eighteenth-century washing bowl, Iranian.
PINEAPPLE & GINGER POLL	Byron's Complete Works (nineteenth-century edition).
POM POM	Iris.
PURPLE HAZE	Mixed Cape Greens.
PURPLE ORCHID	*Cymbidium* (Orchid).
RASPBERRY MILK	Red and white *kaffiyeh* (male Arab headdress); white cord *agal*, with which the headdress is secured.
RED AXE	Nineteenth-century Arabian dagger; *Anthurium andreanum* (Painter's Palette).
ROSEWATER	Omani ceremonial *Khanjar*; *Rosa* (Hybrid Tea).
ST CLEMENTS	Mixed Cape Greens.
SHARP START	Top of an antique Arabian censer; chess piece.
STRAWBERRY ROYALE	*Cymbidium* (Orchid).
SUMMER-SET	Mixed Cape Greens.

SUNRISE   Earthenware jug.

TONGA   Oriental decorated eggs.

TYRE TEA   Lebanese coffee pot; Mahgrebian camel bag, c.1930; Mesopotamian copper water bottle, c.1920.

UGLI   *Tropaeolum majus* (Nasturtium).

Royal Brierley's Braemar Jug appears on pages 84, 114, 117; the Chartwell Footed Bowl on page 100; the Cornflower Honey Pot on pages 21, 45, 80, 117; the Coventry Jug on page 58; the Footed Bud Vase on page 107; the Fuschia Martini and Swizzle on page 37; the Gainsborough Jug on pages 11, 91; the Heart-shaped Chartwell Perfume on page 20; the Honeysuckle Footed Bowl on page 88; and the Viceroy Wine Decanter on page 11.

INDEX TO COCKTAIL TYPES